J B N736 12
Dunn, Joeming W.
Richard Nixon : 37th U.S.
president

111011

Presidents of the United States Bio-Graphics

Richard Nixon
37th U.S. President

Written by **Joeming Dunn**   Illustrated by **Ben Dunn**

magic
Wagon

visit us at www.abdopublishing.com

 This book contains at least 10% recycled materials.

Written by Joeming Dunn
Illustrated by Ben Dunn
Colored by Robby Bevard
Lettered by Doug Dlin
Edited by Stephanie Hedlund and Rochelle Baltzer
Interior layout and design by Antarctic Press
Cover art by Ben Dunn
Cover design by Abbey Fitzgerald

Library of Congress Cataloging-in-Publication Data

Dunn, Joeming W.
  Richard Nixon : 37th U.S. president / written by Joeming Dunn ; illustrated by Ben Dunn.
     p. cm. -- (Presidents of the United States bio-graphics)
  Includes index.
  ISBN 978-1-61641-647-8
  1. Nixon, Richard M. (Richard Milhous), 1913-1994--Juvenile literature. 2. Presidents--United States--Biography--Juvenile literature. 3. Nixon, Richard M. (Richard Milhous), 1913-1994--Comic books, strips, etc. 4. Presidents--United States--Biography--Comic books, strips, etc. 5. Graphic novels. I. Dunn, Ben, ill. II. Title.
  E856.D86 2012
  973.924092--dc22
  [B]   2011010674

Table of Contents

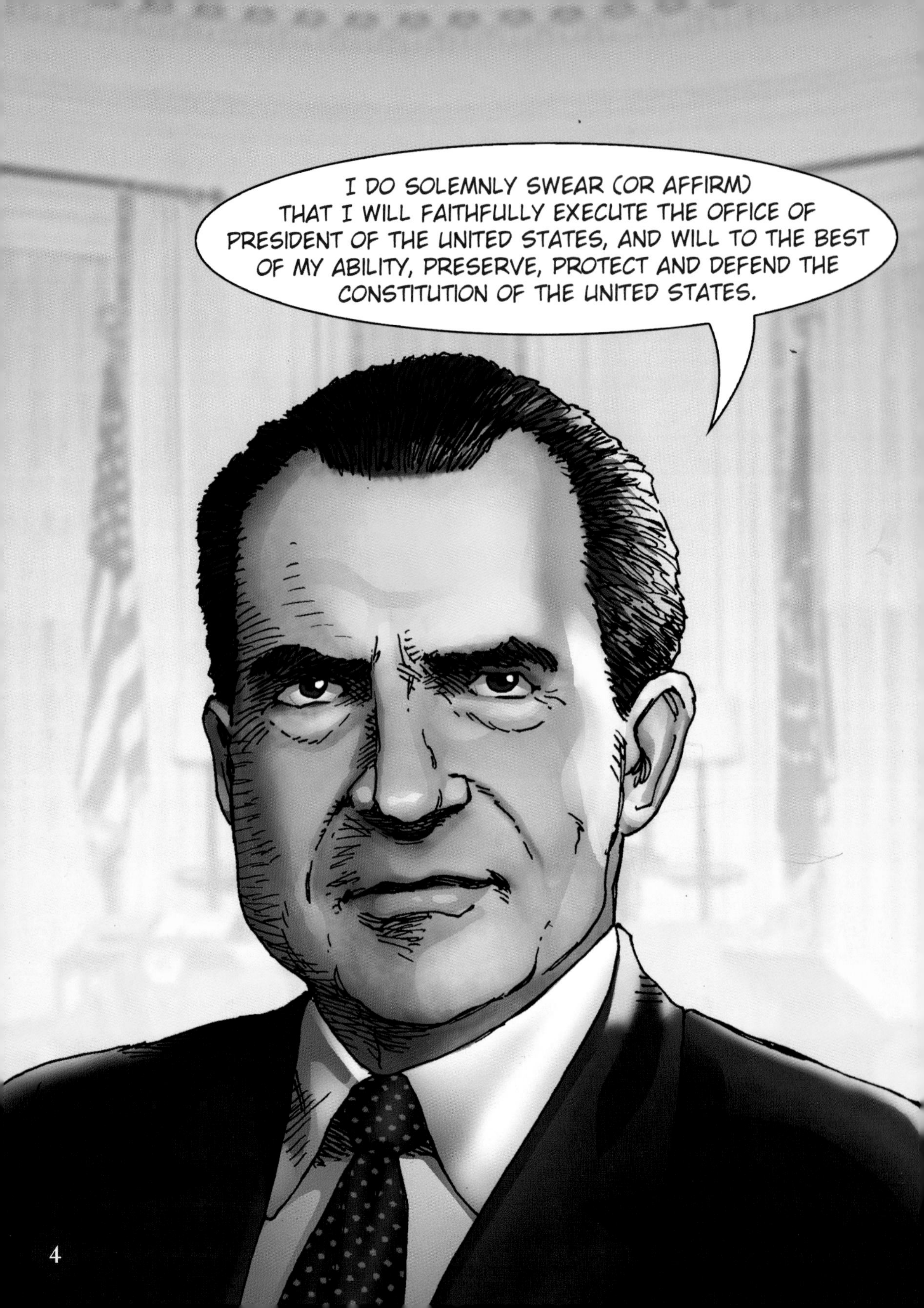
I DO SOLEMNLY SWEAR (OR AFFIRM) THAT I WILL FAITHFULLY EXECUTE THE OFFICE OF PRESIDENT OF THE UNITED STATES, AND WILL TO THE BEST OF MY ABILITY, PRESERVE, PROTECT AND DEFEND THE CONSTITUTION OF THE UNITED STATES.

Richard Milhous Nixon was born on January 9, 1913, in Yorba Linda, California. He was the second of five children.

His mother, Hannah Milhous Nixon, was a Quaker. This was a big part of Richard's childhood.

When Richard was nine years old, the Nixon family moved. His father opened a service station in Whittier, California.

FULL SERVICE STATION
FLATS FIXED
OIL CHANGE

GA

Richard helped around the store whenever he could.

IS THERE ANYTHING ELSE I CAN DO FOR YOU?

Nixon attended Whittier College, a Quaker institution. He graduated in 1934.

He then attended Duke University School of Law. He graduated third in his class in 1937.

After graduation, Nixon returned to Whittier. He joined a small law practice. He then met Thelma "Pat" Ryan while both were performing in a local community play.

They married on June 21, 1940. Together they had two children.

On December 7, 1941, the Japanese attacked Pearl Harbor, Hawaii. This was the beginning of World War II for America.

Due to the war, many things were rationed. Nixon went to Washington DC and worked in the tire rationing division.

OFFICE OF PRICE ADMINISTRATION

In 1942, Nixon joined the U.S. Navy. He served in the Naval Air Transport Command. Nixon soon reached the rank of lieutenant commander.

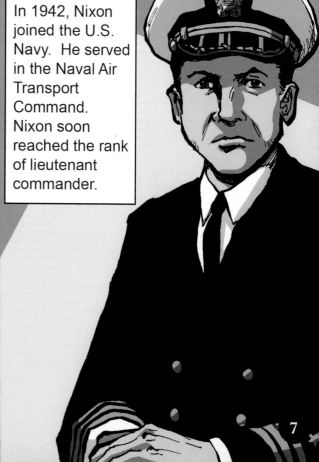

After the war, Nixon was known for his leadership in the Navy. Many people pushed Nixon to run for U.S. Congress. He ran against Democrat Jerry Voorhis.

Nixon said Voorhis had Communist beliefs. This was not proven, but the attack led to Nixon's victory in 1946. He was also reelected in 1948.

Nixon was assigned to the House Un-American Activities Committee. Its purpose was to find Communists in the government.

One of the committee's more high-profile cases involved Alger Hiss.

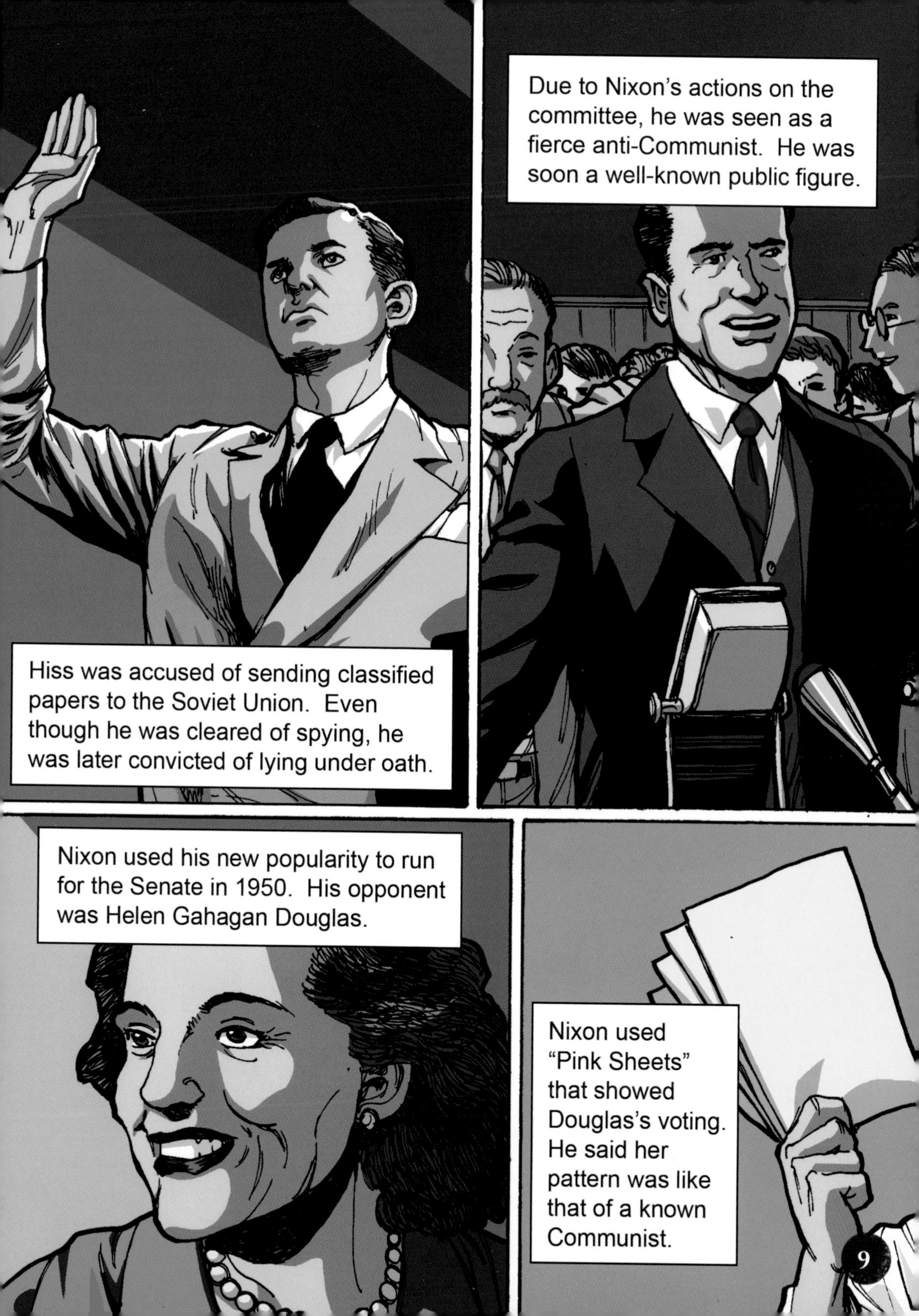
Hiss was accused of sending classified papers to the Soviet Union. Even though he was cleared of spying, he was later convicted of lying under oath.
Due to Nixon's actions on the committee, he was seen as a fierce anti-Communist. He was soon a well-known public figure.
Nixon used his new popularity to run for the Senate in 1950. His opponent was Helen Gahagan Douglas.
Nixon used "Pink Sheets" that showed Douglas's voting. He said her pattern was like that of a known Communist.

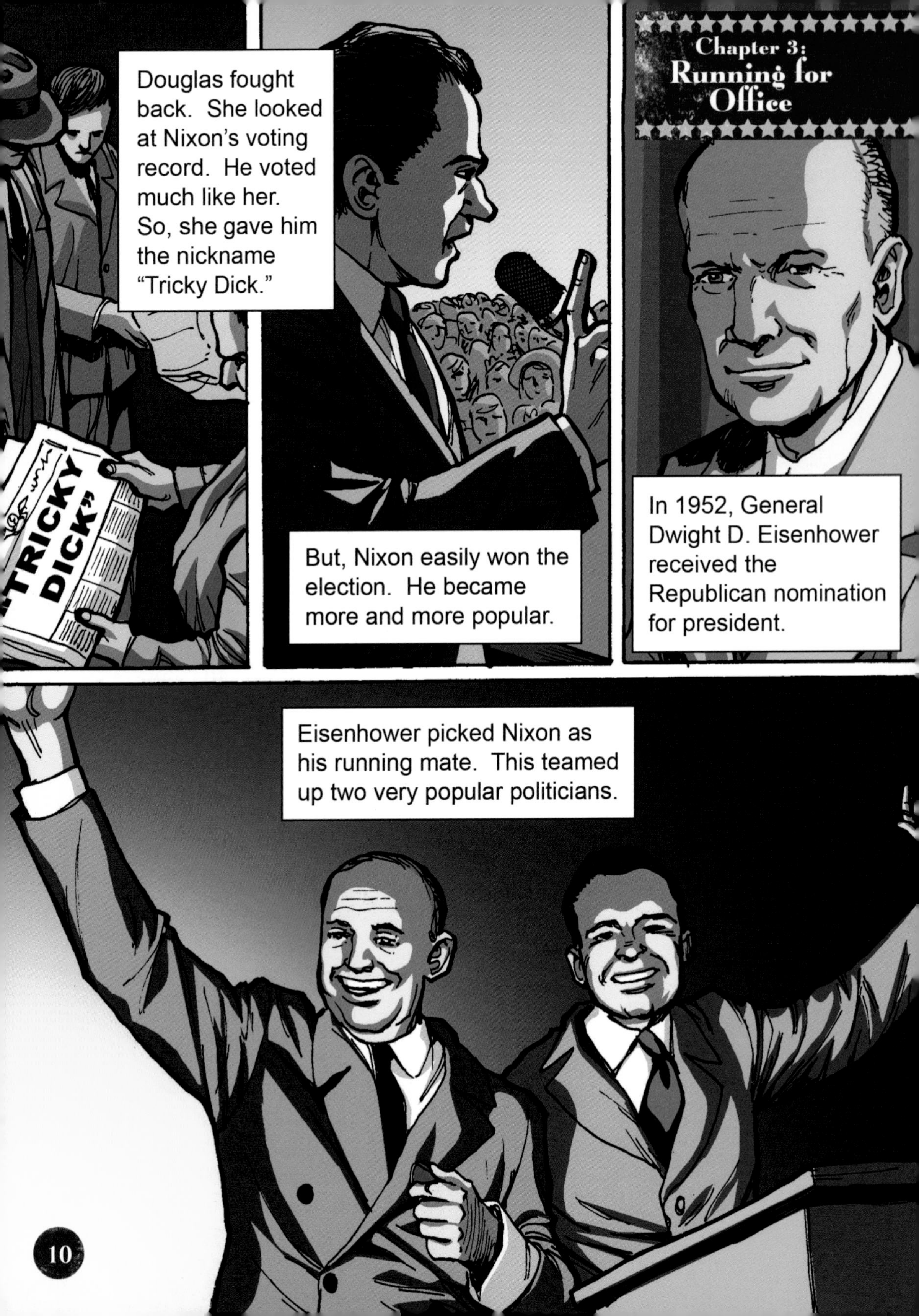
Douglas fought back. She looked at Nixon's voting record. He voted much like her. So, she gave him the nickname "Tricky Dick."
"TRICKY DICK"
But, Nixon easily won the election. He became more and more popular.
Chapter 3: Running for Office
In 1952, General Dwight D. Eisenhower received the Republican nomination for president.
Eisenhower picked Nixon as his running mate. This teamed up two very popular politicians.

Almost immediately, the campaign had problems. The *New York Post* reported that Nixon had a "slush fund."

The paper said wealthy Californians were giving money to get favors from Nixon.

On September 23, 1952, Nixon appeared on national television. He admitted there was a fund, but he said that it was not used improperly. He gave information on where the money came from and how it was used.

Nixon did admit to keeping one gift. It was a cocker spaniel that his six-year-old daughter named Checkers.

REGARDLESS OF WHAT THEY SAY, WE ARE GOING TO KEEP IT.

YOU'RE MY BOY.

Nixon originally thought the speech was a failure. But it was a success.

Eisenhower and Nixon easily won. They defeated Democratic candidate Adlai Stevenson and his running mate, John Sparkman.

The two also won reelection in 1956.

FOR PRESIDENT FOR VICE-PRESIDENT

DWIGHT D. EISENHOWER RICHARD M. NIXON

DICK
SURE TO CLICK

ICAN AIRLI

As vice president, Nixon traveled around the world to represent the United States.

Nixon mostly used these trips to get support for America's Cold War policies. He was met with mixed reactions. On a trip to Caracas, Venezuela, protesters threw rocks at Nixon's car.

In March 1957, Nixon visited Libya for a program of economic and military aid.

In July 1959, he went to the Soviet Union. As vice president, Nixon also officially opened the 1960 Winter Olympics in California.

Nixon easily received the Republican nomination for president in 1960.

His opponent was Democratic senator John F. Kennedy from Massachusetts.

This campaign would be different than previous ones. The television era was beginning, and the two candidates agreed to a series of four televised debates.

Nixon did not use makeup during the debates. He looked pale and ill compared to a youthful Kennedy.

Many believed the television debates cost Nixon the election. He lost by less than 115,000 popular votes.

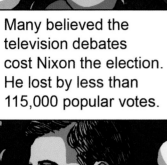

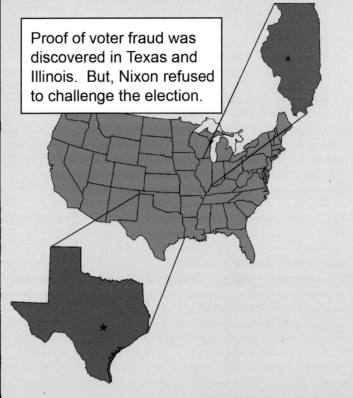

Proof of voter fraud was discovered in Texas and Illinois. But, Nixon refused to challenge the election.

Nixon returned to California. There, he joined a Los Angeles law firm and wrote a book called *Six Crises*.

RICHARD M. NIXON

SIX CRISES

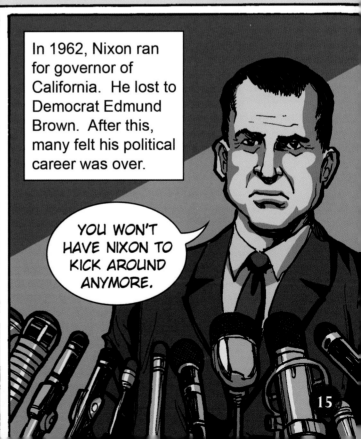

In 1962, Nixon ran for governor of California. He lost to Democrat Edmund Brown. After this, many felt his political career was over.

YOU WON'T HAVE NIXON TO KICK AROUND ANYMORE.

Nixon did not keep his promise for long. In 1968, he ran for president again.

Nixon ran against Democrat Hubert Humphrey and third-party candidate George Wallace.

Nixon easily defeated both candidates. In 1969, he became the 37th president of the United States.

In his first year in office, Nixon saw Kennedy's dream of landing a man on the moon come true.

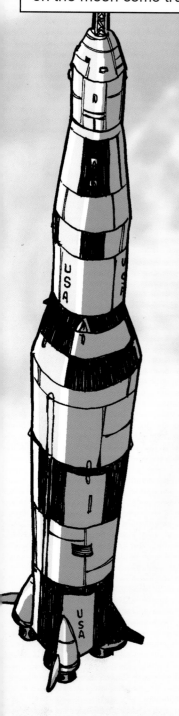

After the launch of *Apollo 11*, Nixon talked to astronauts Neil Armstrong and Buzz Aldrin. It became the longest long-distance phone call ever.

Because of Nixon, NASA was able to begin development of the space shuttle.

Nixon also signed a law that lowered the voting age from 21 to 18. This law eventually became the 26th Amendment to the Constitution.

Nixon tried to fight these problems by changing how the dollar was measured. He didn't want the dollar to be equal to a certain amount of gold.

At the time of his election, the country was going through a recession. There were high unemployment rates and inflation.

He also set wage and price freezes.

At first this helped the economy. But, it did not keep inflation from rising.

OUT
WOR
PLEA
HEL

Nixon did start many changes in welfare, civil rights, and environmental causes.

He introduced laws for Supplemental Security Income (SSI).

SSI provides benefits for the disabled. It also established automatic cost of living adjustments (COLA) for people who receive Social Security.

Nixon helped create the Environmental Protection Agency (EPA) to help protect the environment.

He also helped create the Occupational Safety and Health Administration (OSHA) to help protect workers.

He also began mandatory desegregation of public places...

SCHOOL

...and instructed that federal construction projects have a certain percentage of jobs for minorities.

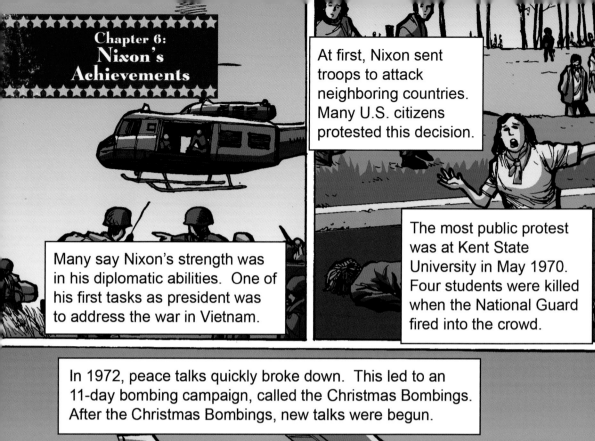

At first, Nixon sent troops to attack neighboring countries. Many U.S. citizens protested this decision.

Many say Nixon's strength was in his diplomatic abilities. One of his first tasks as president was to address the war in Vietnam.

The most public protest was at Kent State University in May 1970. Four students were killed when the National Guard fired into the crowd.

In 1972, peace talks quickly broke down. This led to an 11-day bombing campaign, called the Christmas Bombings. After the Christmas Bombings, new talks were begun.

A peace treaty was signed in January 1973. This led to the withdrawal of American troops and the end of the war.

One of Nixon's most important achievements was to reconnect with the People's Republic of China. The United States and China had been at odds for 20 years.

During the 1940s, the Nationalist Chinese government fled to Taiwan during a civil war. The United States supported the Nationalist government in Taiwan as separate. But mainland China believed they were one country.

Nixon sent National Security Advisor Henry Kissinger for secret talks to mainland China.

The talks had begun thanks to visits by the table tennis teams from each country. So, talks were called "ping-pong diplomacy."

In February 1972, Nixon visited mainland China.

The U.S. talks with China led to the country being included in the United Nations.

The improving relations with China opened the doors for talks with the Soviet Union.

Nixon visited the Soviet Union and its leader, Premier Leonid Brezhnev, in May 1972.

WE SHALL SOMETIMES BE COMPETITORS, BUT WE NEED NEVER BE ENEMIES.

Nixon and Brezhnev's talks led to the first Strategic Arms and Limitation Talks (SALT I). These talks were the first step in nuclear arms reduction.

Some would say one of Nixon's diplomatic failures was the Yom Kippur War in 1973. It was the fourth war between Syria and Egypt against Israel.

When the United States supported Israel in the war, many Arab countries were upset.

The countries stopped oil from leaving many oil-producing nations in the Middle East. This led to the 1973 Oil Crisis.

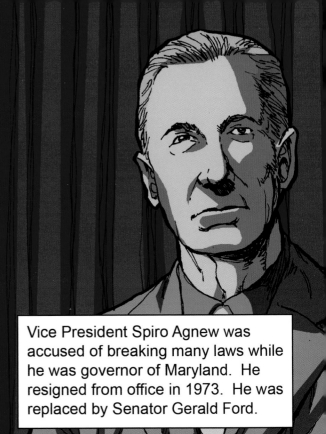

Nixon and his running mate, Spiro Agnew, easily won reelection in 1972. Soon after, Nixon's Administration was hit with scandal.

Vice President Spiro Agnew was accused of breaking many laws while he was governor of Maryland. He resigned from office in 1973. He was replaced by Senator Gerald Ford.

While campaigning for his second term, Nixon had formed a committee for the campaign. It was called the Committee to Re-elect the President (CREEP).

After the arrests, Nixon supposedly began a cover-up. He was said to have told White House counsel John Dean to make secret payments to the burglars. These payments were to prevent them from naming the Administration.

In June 1972, five burglars working for CREEP had been arrested. They were breaking into the Democratic National Headquarters at the Watergate Complex. They were there to gather information and place wiretaps.

Two reporters from the *Washington Post*, Carl Bernstein and Bob Woodward, investigated the possible cover-up. Their source, called "Deep Throat," showed the cover-up reached the Oval Office.

In February 1973, a special Senate committee was formed to investigate the Watergate affair.

Many of Nixon's inner circle resigned, including Chief of Staff H.R. Haldeman, Special Assistant John Ehrlichman, and Attorney General Richard Kleindienst.

During the hearings, it was discovered that Nixon had an Oval Office taping system installed in 1969. A request for the tapes was made. But Nixon refused to produce them. Many began to wonder what the president knew.

Chapter 8

Nixon Resigns

I AM NOT A CROOK.

With pressure mounting, Nixon gave a news conference. At that time, he released seven of the nine tapes requested.

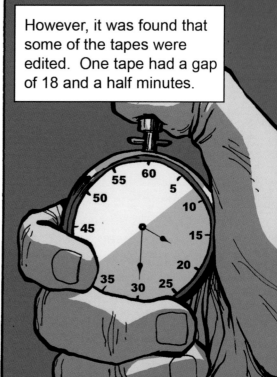

However, it was found that some of the tapes were edited. One tape had a gap of 18 and a half minutes.

The House Judiciary Committee recommended impeachment. Their reasons were abuse of power, obstruction of justice, and failure to comply with subpoenas.

Facing near-certain impeachment, Nixon announced his resignation on August 8, 1974. He became the first president of the United States to resign.

After Nixon's resignation, Vice President Gerald Ford became president. He pardoned Nixon of any crimes associated with Watergate on September 8, 1974.

After resigning, Nixon and his wife moved to California. He wrote several books, including *RN: The Memoirs of Richard Nixon* and *Beyond Peace*.

These books helped recover his image from the scandal.

He remained in the background of politics. But he still gave advice to Presidents George H.W. Bush and Bill Clinton.

Nixon passed away on April 22, 1994, of a massive stroke. He was buried at the Nixon Library in Yorba Linda, California.

Name - Richard Milhous Nixon   Born - January 9, 1913

Wife - Thelma "Pat" Ryan (1912–1993)   Children - 2

Political Party - Republican

Age at Inauguration - 56   Years Served - 1969–1974

Vice Presidents - Spiro T. Agnew, Gerald Ford

Died - April 22, 1994, 81 years old

President Nixon's Cabinet

First term - January 20, 1969–January 20, 1973
• State – William P. Rogers

• Treasury – David M. Kennedy, John B. Connally Jr. (from February 11, 1971), George P. Shultz (from June 12, 1972)

• Defense – Melvin R. Laird

• Attorney General – John N. Mitchell, Richard G. Kleindienst (from June 12, 1972)

• Interior – Walter J. Hickel, Rogers C.B. Morton (from January 29, 1971)

• Agriculture – Clifford M. Hardin, Earl L. Butz (from December 2, 1971)

• Commerce – Maurice H. Stans, Peter G. Peterson (from February 21, 1972)

• Labor – George P. Shultz, James D. Hodgson (from July 2, 1970)

• Health, Education, and Welfare – Robert H. Finch, Elliot L. Richardson (from June 24, 1970)

• Housing and Urban Development – George W. Romney

• Transportation – John A. Volpe

Second term - January 20, 1973–August 9, 1974
• State – William P. Rogers, Henry A. Kissinger (from September 22, 1973)

• Treasury – George P. Shultz, William E. Simon (from May 8, 1974)

• Defense – Elliot L. Richardson, James R. Schlesinger (from July 2, 1973)

• Attorney General – Richard G. Kleindienst, Elliot L. Richardson (from May 25, 1973), William B. Saxbe (from January 4, 1974)

• Interior – Rogers C.B. Morton

• Agriculture – Earl L. Butz

• Commerce – Frederick B. Dent

• Labor – Peter J. Brennan

• Health, Education, and Welfare – Caspar W. Weinberger

• Housing and Urban Development – James T. Lynn

• Transportation – Claude S. Brinegar

• To be president, a person must meet three requirements. He or she must be at least 35 years old and a natural-born U.S. citizen. A candidate must also have lived in the United States for at least 14 years.

• The U.S. presidential election is an indirect election. Voters from each state elect representatives called electors for the Electoral College. The number of electors is based on population. Each elector pledges to cast their vote for the candidate who receives the highest number of popular votes in their state. A candidate must receive the majority of Electoral College votes to win.

• Each president may be elected to two four-year terms. The presidential election is held on the Tuesday after the first Monday in November. The president is sworn in on January 20 of the following year.

• While in office, the president receives a salary of $400,000 each year. He or she lives in the White House and has 24-hour Secret Service protection. When the president leaves office, he or she receives Secret Service protection for ten more years. He or she also receives a yearly pension of $191,300 and funding for office space, supplies, and staff.

Timeline

1913 - Richard Milhous Nixon was born on January 9 in Yorba Linda, California.

1937 - Nixon graduated third in his class at Duke University School of Law.

1940 - Nixon married Thelma "Pat" Ryan on June 21.

1942 - Nixon joined the U.S. Navy.

1946 - Nixon was elected to Congress.

1952 - Eisenhower was nominated for president and picked Nixon as his running mate; Eisenhower and Nixon won the election.

1956 - Eisenhower and Nixon were reelected to a second term.

1960 - Nixon was nominated for president; he narrowly lost the election.

1962 - Nixon lost the California race for governor.

1968 - Nixon ran for president and defeated Wallace and Humphrey.

1972 - The Watergate burglars were arrested in June; Nixon won reelection in November; Bernstein and Woodward uncovered the Watergate conspiracy.

1973 - A Senate committee was formed in February to investigate the Watergate affair; in October, Agnew resigned from vice presidency.

1974 - The House Judiciary Committee opened impeachment hearings on Nixon; on August 8, Nixon resigned from the presidency; on September 8, Ford pardoned Nixon.

1994 - Nixon died of a stroke on April 22.

Web Sites

To learn more about Richard Nixon, visit ABDO Publishing Group online at **www.abdopublishing.com**. Web sites about Nixon are featured on our Book Links page. These links are routinely monitored and updated to provide the most current information available.

Glossary

campaign - to give speeches and state ideas in order to be voted into an elected office.

classified - kept from the public in order to protect national security.

Cold War - a period of tension and hostility between the United States and its allies and the Soviet Union and its allies after World War II.

communism - a social and economic system in which everything is owned by the government and given to the people as needed. A person who believes in communism is called a communist.

cost of living - the average cost of goods and services necessary to maintain a standard lifestyle. In countries with a high cost of living, goods and services are expensive.

debate - a contest in which two sides argue for or against something.

Democrat - a member of the Democratic political party. Democrats believe in social change and strong government.

desegregation - to free of any law or practice that keeps the members of a particular race in separate units.

diplomacy - the practice of handling discussions and compromises between nations.

impeach - to charge a public official for crime or misconduct in office.

inflation - a rise in the price of goods and services.

minority - a racial, religious, or political group that differs from a larger group in a population.

nuclear arms - weapons powered by nuclear energy. Nuclear energy is created when atoms are divided or combined.

obstruction of justice - the crime of interfering with the police or the justice system in a legal case.

pardon - to free a person from punishment for an offense.

Quaker - a member of the religious group called the Society of Friends. Quakers believe in simple manners and clothes, and they oppose war.

ration - a fixed amount of food or goods that are scarce.

recession - a time when business activity slows.

Republican - a member of the Republican political party. Republicans are conservative and believe in small government.

running mate - a candidate running for a lower-rank position on an election ticket, especially the candidate for vice president.

scandal - an action that shocks people and disgraces those connected with it.

subpoena - a document commanding the person named in it to appear at court.

Vietnam War - from 1957 to 1975. A long, failed attempt by the United States to stop North Vietnam from taking over South Vietnam.

Index